D1706433

"Thank you" to Bríg Rose, my family, and friends for their support. Adobe Firefly for visuals, and artificial intelligence (Chat GPT and Google Bard) for dialogue assistance.

Chapter 1

In the fifth dimension, there is a place that transcends the linear confines of time. The air is a million shades of blue, purple, and silver. Only sparks of floating light exist there. Crystal towers grow from their thoughts while bridges of light connect floating islands. At the heart of these islands is a massive crystal spiral that contains an energy vortex. This vortex serves as a connecting point between dimensions.

In a crystal pod, a violet light gazes with concern at the holographic display of the third dimension. As the violet light contemplates, a nearby blue light telepathically says, "Remember, they are still immature in their spiritual development. They are like little children. Their wants bound them to that dimension."

The violet light sighs, "I suppose. But it is frustrating watching them repeat the same patterns. You would think they would get tired." The violet light pauses as a memory surfaces, "My mom once shared a tale of a great divide. In the past, our dimension was a single and harmonious island. We all worked together to raise our consciousness as we do today. However, discord arose, leading to a decline in our collective awareness. Some lights among us began to change, taking on shades of green, orange, and red. Their desires veered toward permanence–a solid existence."

The violet light dims with sadness, "Initially, we tried to guide them towards balance, but their passions grew stronger. They manifested a solidness that shattered our dimension. We were fragmented into the scattered islands we now inhabit. These were the beings who fell into the third dimension. There, they are worshiped and regarded as the elite. Those beings in the third dimension are unaware of their true intentions. They trust them implicitly, failing to question their motives. If only they would delve into their history, they would realize the truth."

An indigo light approaches, "Mom, what's wrong?"

The violet light flickers with weariness. "I have watched this dimension for so long. I fear that the beings have chosen to evolve for their gain instead of becoming better. Their decision is fine, as this is their choice. However, what about those younger people? Shouldn't they have a chance? Should they suffer because of the older ones?"

The indigo light says, "Mom, you're allowing your light to dim as you take on their pain. You aren't saying what is happening. Can you expand on what you see?"

The violet light desperately replies, "It is 2023 down there. I see that they are running out of time to choose. The elite has led billions of occupants to focus on their physical senses. Their plan has always been for immortality. They have succeeded by making a pact with technology. The issue is once the billions have merged with machinery, they will become solid forever. There will be no advancement to dimensions such as ours."

"Do you believe there are any beings left you can reach before this happens?" The indigo light compassionately asks.

The violet light responds, "Yes, I have watched a being known as Jonathan for at least one thousand years. Every time he gets close to raising his consciousness, he falls backward. He recycles into the same family and social dynamics. However, I believe he can be helped this time. He seems to have retained some information and desires to help others. But if nothing or no one interjects, he will fall backward. However, this time, he will be trapped in that dimension."

"Alright, mom, I will go to that dimension. I will try to help Jonathan by teaching him some of our ways. I know we can't influence the will of another being, as it has to be their choice. So, I will be discreet," the indigo light says.

The violet light, appreciative of her daughter's courage, responds with gratitude. "Thank you. However, since this is a big decision, you must prepare yourself. Go and talk to your inner guide."

The indigo light returns to her soothing crystal pod and connects to her inner guide.

The indigo light receives a vision, "You're about to undertake a significant task. The situation is dire in that realm."

The indigo light responds, "I've only heard about their issues from listening to my mom. I can only imagine how experiencing it firsthand will be different."

"Remember, your purpose will be to bring light and understanding to their reality. Your mere presence will create ripples of positive change. Your energy can act as a catalyst for transformation. Yet, you mustn't forget that you aren't from that dimension."

The indigo light reflects on the guidance of her inner guide. She takes a moment to embrace the light within the crystal pod. She thinks, "I am ready to immerse myself in their world and hopefully be a force for positive change."

She returns to the violet light, "I am prepared for my journey."

The violet light says, "Please be careful. Things are quickly happening in that dimension."

The violet light manifests a crystal cube, "Here are some items you may need down there. If you need anything, focus your thoughts, and whatever you need will appear. You will have physical experiences you aren't used to. I cannot prepare you for them. But remember that I will be here watching you."

The indigo light approaches the crystal vortex and descends into the third dimension.

The violet light watches the holographic display and whispers, "Your journey has a great purpose. Hopefully, you can redirect Jonathan."

An indigo flicker trails across the Chicago sky. It zeroed in on a lone figure strolling down the sidewalk. The indigo light abruptly lands. She quickly manifests a human form and her crystal cube turns into a backpack. She stumbles in front of Jonathan.

Jonathan's eyes widened. He is confused that someone is kneeling at his feet. He looks up to the sky. Before he can utter any words, the indigo light says, giggling, "Clumsy, me."

Jonathan chuckles, "Glad you're okay," he says, extending his hand. "Let me help you up...So, what's your name?"

The indigo light pauses, and she receives a flash within her mind, "Oh, I know. You can call me Indigo."

Jonathan's eyebrows raise, "Indigo? Unusual, but beautiful."

Indigo smiles, "You can say my mom calls me that all the time. Thank you for helping me. What's your name?"

"Jonathan," he replies. He tilts his head, "You seem...familiar. Have we met?"

"No," Indigo quickly responds. "This is my first time in this dimension. I mean city."

Jonathan chuckles, "Yes, you can say the city is another dimension. Would you like coffee? I was heading to that new shop right down the street."

Coffee is an alien concept to Indigo. She searches her mind and receives a flash. "Maybe water instead," she responds.

"They have water," Jonathan remarks. He leads the way to the coffee shop. As they walk into the coffee shop, Indigo sees a glimpse of herself in the glass door. "Oh wow," she mumbles.

Jonathan turns around, "Did you say something?"

"I said, oh wow, look at this shop," Indigo nervously responds.

Jonathan and Indigo sit at a small table. Indigo looks out the window. She sees many cars passing by, and the coffee shop is noisy. She feels overwhelmed and is nervously shaking her legs. Jonathan goes to the counter, orders his coffee, and purchases a cup of water for Indigo.

Jonathan sits down, gives Indigo the cup of water, and asks, "Is everything okay?"

Indigo responds, "Yes, I am new to the city. I guess I didn't realize how busy it would be. The coffee shop is crowded, and the noise playing is loud."

Jonathan asks, "The noise? Do you mean music? Where are you from?"

Indigo is stumped on what to name her dimension but quickly responds, "I am from Serenity Haven. We don't have music there."

Jonathan's eyebrows raise, "Really, they don't have music?" He shakes his head, "I haven't heard of Serenity Haven. Where exactly is that located?"

"It's a tiny group of islands. You can say it is out of this world. It isn't your typical travel destination. I am here on a short mission," Indigo responds.

Jonathan laughs, "You are funny. Do you mean job? How long will you be in Chicago?"

"I have a temporary job that requires some investigative work. Once that job is finished, I can return to Serenity Haven," Indigo replies.

Jonathan goes to the counter and grabs his coffee. He returns to the table and asks, "Would you like to go somewhere less noisy?"

Indigo responds, "Yes, I would love to go somewhere quieter."

Jonathan and Indigo walk to a nearby park by the lake. Indigo says, "Wow, the lake is beautiful."

Jonathan replies, "I come here often to think."

They sit on a park bench. Although Indigo knows Jonathan's life, she asks, "Are you working?"

Jonathan responds, "No, I am currently in between jobs. I haven't been able to focus because my home situation is terrible. I graduated high school a year ago, and living costs are ridiculous, so I live at home. I am going to college and considering joining the military."

"I am sorry about your home life," she sighs. "I have a supportive family. My mom is the one who encouraged me to see life outside of Serenity Haven."

Indigo has a vision, and empathetically says, "Jonathan, I feel the military isn't for you. I could only imagine your home situation. But I don't think that you should join the military…What are you studying at college?"

"I am majoring in psychology," Jonathan sighs as he thinks about his home situation.

Indigo asks, "Psychology. That is good. What do you plan on doing with that major?"

Jonathan's cell phone rings, "Hello. Yes, I am on my way back."

He says agitatedly, "Speaking of home, I need to go watch my younger brother. My mom is overprotective. She's leaving for work, and my stepfather is at work…anyway, is there a way I can get in touch with you?"

She asks, "Yes, what device did you pick up?"

"It's a cell phone. Let me guess, you don't have one of these in Serenity Haven," he says.

Indigo responds, "No, but my mom packed my bag with necessary items. She is more aware of life outside of Serenity Haven." Indigo reaches into her backpack, and pulls out a cell phone, "See, I told you my mom would know the items I needed."

Jonathan gives Indigo his phone number, "Call my phone, and then I will save your phone number."

She pauses and quickly gains information on how to use the phone. She calls his phone and hangs up.

Jonathan says, "I will give you a call so we can continue our talk. I enjoy being around you. You have such a beautiful smile."

"I am known to be cheerful," Indigo smiles.

"Be careful in Chicago. Remember, this isn't Serenity Haven," he says as he walks away.

Indigo looks down, "Yes, you are right."

She walks back to the coffee shop. As she approaches the counter to order, an unexpected wave of hunger washes over her. She mutters, "Ugh, I didn't expect to have the physical needs of the third dimension. I think I am hungry."

She scans the menu and thinks, "I don't understand these items." She receives a flash of vegetables. She orders a vegetarian wrap and realizes she might need to use the bathroom.

She walks into the bathroom and stands in front of the mirror. She stares intently at her reflection. The bathroom door swings open, and Indigo gazes at the person. The young lady says, "What are you looking at?"

Indigo closes her eyes, takes a deep breath, and thinks, "Did I do something wrong?"

Indigo enters the stall and uses the toilet. Afterward, Indigo glances at the same woman and sees her waving her hand near the faucet. Indigo waves her hand and gets chills from the cold water. She thinks, "How can I get used to this?"

Indigo walks out of the bathroom and sits at a table. She looks up and sees a screen with the world news. Various scenes of chaos on earth flicker with wars, earthquakes, homelessness, and poverty. It appears that chaos is spreading like a wildfire.

Indigo mumbles, "No wonder they are struggling."

The cashier calls her name. Indigo walks to the counter and is grateful for the food. She thanks the cashier and takes her vegetarian wrap. She sits down and continues to reflect on the conditions of the third dimension. A tear falls from her eyes, and she mumbles, "This is strange."

Indigo quickly eats, leaves the coffee shop, and realizes it's getting dark.

She looks around, "Where will I sleep?" She sees an alleyway and decides to make a crystal pod. Using her thoughts a crystal pod appears instantly. "This should keep me warm." Indigo enters the invisible pod.

From her backpack, Indigo pulls out a notebook and a violet blanket, "Thanks, mom. You knew I would need something to express my thoughts."

Indigo recalls all the day's events, including the horrific scenes of global devastation on the news. She remembers her conversation with her spirit guide and writes in her journal, "Today is my first day in Chicago. I realize the intensity of the physical senses within this dimension."

She mumbles, "It is easy to become distracted by hunger or even using the bathroom. I think the young lady in the bathroom was offended. She didn't realize that I meant nothing by the stare. Then their news is overwhelming."

Indigo continues to write, "The chaos is substantial here. How are they supposed to grow when things are constantly thrown at them?"

Indigo closes her journal and wraps herself in the blanket. "Mom, I am sending you my love."

Indigo's mom looks through the holographic display, "I know you can't hear me, but I am sending you my love also. You did exceptionally well on your first day. Thank you."

The next morning, Indigo's cell phone rings, interrupting her contemplation. She answers, "Hello."

On the other end, Jonathan's voice is uplifting, "Morning Indigo. Why are you whispering?"

Indigo responds, "I was journaling."

"Well, you want to meet at the park in two hours?" Jonathan asks, hoping Indigo would say yes.

Indigo's eyes brighten, "Yes, I would."

After they hang up, Indigo continues to journal. She is optimistic the day will be better. She dematerializes her sleeping area and begins her walk to the park. As she's walking out of the alley, she sees two men in a heated dispute over a parking space. She looks around and sees another vacant parking spot.

As Indigo is about to interrupt, she senses her mother. The violet light watches Indigo through the holographic display and telepathically says, "I know it's painful to watch Indigo, but do not get distracted or discouraged. You'll encounter behaviors that may bring you pain. But always remember, your mission is to assist Jonathan. Engaging in their conflicts and desires will weaken your abilities and eventually trap you in their density."

Indigo has a sudden revelation that intervening in their argument may not be the best action. Taking a deep breath, she continues her journey to the park. The memory of the bathroom incident from the day before resurfaces in her thoughts. She can't help but think, "It's another day, but it feels like déjà vu."

When Indigo arrives at the park, she spots Jonathan sitting on a nearby bench. As she approaches, he greets her with a warm smile. "Hey, Indigo. It's great to see you again. How's everything?"

Indigo sighs and begins to recount her recent experiences. "Yesterday, I returned to the coffee shop to get something to eat. But, while I was there, a woman took offense and spoke to me rather harshly. I closed my eyes and took a deep breath in an attempt to understand what I did wrong. Then, as I was waiting for my food, I watched the news. There was chaos and strife all around. On my way here, two men were locked in a heated argument over a parking space. The anger and tension here are so different from Serenity Haven."

Jonathan nods his head. "Yeah, Chicago has its challenges. Life can be tough for many people here. Yesterday, I mentioned that if I had a choice I wouldn't live here."

Indigo responds, "My mom packed a journal. So, I journaled last night and this morning,"

"Yes, you did say something about journaling when we spoke earlier."

Indigo says, "Journaling isn't something we typically do in Serenity Haven. We prefer to communicate in ways that promote growth and seek peaceful resolutions."

Jonathan remarks, "That's different from this city. In many of these communities, people aren't encouraging growth for one another."

"Wow, that is sad," Indigo replies.

Jonathan says, "Sometimes people react aggressively to protect themselves. For example, the woman in the bathroom. She reacted aggressively towards you." Jonathan reaches into his backpack and pulls out old bread. He smiles and says, "Would you like to feed the birds? Instead of wasting the bread, I prefer feeding it to them."

Indigo and Jonathan walk around the park and feed the birds. Just as they finish, Jonathan's phone rings, and it's his mom.

"I apologize, Indigo," Jonathan says, slightly agitated. "My mom and stepfather are expecting me home." He brightens up and suggests, "How about we meet next Saturday? We can visit the botanical gardens?"

Indigo enthusiastically responds, "I'd love to go to the botanical gardens."

"Great," Jonathan smiles. "I'll see you next Saturday."

As Jonathan walks away, Indigo spends more time sitting on a park bench. After a few hours, she returns to the alley. She looks around and manifests her crystal pod. She lies on her blanket and pulls out her journal. She smiles and writes, "Today was challenging as I witnessed people's anger. Yet, Jonathan's kindness in sharing the bread with the birds reminds me that not all hearts have hardened." With her journal entry complete, Indigo closes her journal.

Chapter 2

The following Saturday, Jonathan turns over in bed to look at his clock; he mumbles, "One more week before summer break."

He considers the last two conversations with Indigo and anxiously anticipates seeing her. Jonathan gets dressed and enters the kitchen to prepare breakfast for his family. As Jonathan is cooking, he listens to "Slippin" by DMX. His mom, stepfather, and little brother, Ethan, walk into the kitchen.

Ethan says excitedly, "Good morning, J. Wow, what's all of this?"

"Nothing. I am in a good mood this morning. I wanted to do something nice to get everyone's Saturday started in the right direction," Jonathan replies.

His stepfather says sternly, "Did you cut the grass and clean the bathroom like I asked you yesterday?"

Jonathan says emphatically, "Yes. I've cleaned the entire house, and I will cut the grass after we eat breakfast."

"Good, it's about time you are more productive around here. Turn that music off. No one wants to hear that noise early in the morning," his stepfather grumbles.

Jonathan turns off the music and prepares the plates. His family sits around the table.

Jonathan has two plates of food in his hands. His mom says, "I'm not hungry this morning. I'll just have a couple slices of turkey bacon and orange juice."

Slightly disappointed he says, "Okay mom." He places the plates of food in front of his little brother and stepfather.

Ethan says, "Thanks, J."

"You're welcome," Jonathan replies.

Ethan continues, "Mom, you don't know what you are missing! Jonathan fixed pancakes…"

Before he could finish, his mother said disparagingly, "I see what's on your plate. I don't need you to give me a description!"

Jonathan returns to the table with his mother's turkey bacon on a saucer and places it in front of her. He retrieves the glasses of orange juice and places them in front of his brother and parents. He returns to the counter to get his plate and orange juice and sits down.

The room is awkwardly quiet. Despite his mom's initial refusal of pancakes, she gets up, cuts one of the extra pancakes in half, and eats it. After breakfast, Jonathan washes the dishes. He tells Ethan to get dressed and to meet him outside in 30 minutes to help him cut the grass. Ethan walks into the backyard. He hears Jonathan say as he hangs up the phone, "I look forward to seeing you later."

Ethan's voice, filled with curiosity, asks, "Who was that? I thought we were hanging out today."

Jonathan enthusiastically replies, "That was the young lady I met last weekend."

Ethan remarks sarcastically, "Oh, a girl."

Jonathan looks at Ethan while shaking his head, "It's nothing like that. We are just friends. Her name is Indigo. I don't know why, but I feel my life is about to change."

Ethan asks, "So, when can I meet…"

"Woah, we are just getting to know each other," Jonathan interrupts. "But maybe one day soon, since she is temporarily in Chicago working."

Jonathan and his brother cut the grass, which takes a few hours. Jonathan takes the opportunity to teach his brother how to edge the grass and set the timer for the sprinklers. Afterward, they put away the lawn equipment and returned to the house. Jonathan takes a quick shower and gets dressed for his meeting with Indigo. It's almost 11 o'clock, and they plan to meet at noon at the Botanical Garden in Grant Park.

Jonathan arrives at the Botanical Garden a little earlier than expected, feeling a mix of anticipation and excitement. He finds a bench with a view of people walking towards the entrance. He sits on a bench and waits for Indigo.

Meanwhile, Indigo stops by the coffee shop and purchases a bottle of water. She places the water in her backpack and decides to use the restroom. While she is in the stall, two young women walk into the bathroom. They are standing in front of the mirror, fixing their hair and clothes. They begin to talk.

The taller one says, "Hey girl, how does this new outfit look?"

The other woman replies, "I like the outfit! But I think you should have gotten a different color."

The taller woman asks offendedly, "What's wrong with the color?"

"Nothing girl. Except all you wear is blue. If I didn't know you, I would almost think you wore the same clothes every day," she responds.

She smirked, "Awe, you are right. I need to change that up. I can't have people thinking I don't change my clothes."

The two women laugh, hug, and walk out of the restroom. At that moment, Indigo walks out of the stall. She washes and dries her hands. As she's walking out of the bathroom, she notices her clothing in the mirror. Reflecting on the conversation, she thinks, "It seems as if what you wear is important here."

Realizing she is wearing the same clothing as the previous week. Indigo closes and opens her eyes. She is now wearing a different outfit. Indigo looks in the mirror and smiles. She walks out of the bathroom and leaves the coffee shop.

Indigo planned to walk to the Botanical Garden. But, when she looks at the time, she realizes she will be late. Indigo steps into the alleyway and teleports herself to the Botanical Garden. She reappears just a few feet behind where Jonathan is sitting.

"There you are," she says.

Jonathan turns around. To his amazement, Indigo is walking towards him. Jonathan smiles awkwardly and, with a confused look, asks, "How did you get over there?"

Indigo looks at Jonathan and smiles, "Oh, I just popped in."

Jonathan stands up and walks toward Indigo, "nice outfit."

"Thank you, it is something I made appear," Indigo chuckles.

Jonathan is confused by the statement but doesn't say anything. They begin walking down the pathway. As they walk, Indigo asks, "I remember the first day I met you. You said your home situation was difficult. Can you tell me more about the situation?"

Jonathan replies, "It's nothing."

Indigo says, "Please share. I am interested in your life."

Jonathan takes a moment to reflect on his life. He realizes that Indigo sincerely wants to know more about his life. He thinks about how his family dynamics changed after his father died eight years ago... For the first time, he thinks about how hard it must have been for his mother to raise him and Ethan alone. He looks to the sky and closes his eyes. Jonathan takes a moment to compose himself. He finds a bench, and they sit down.

He takes a deep breath and says, "From birth, until I was seven, things seemed perfect. My parents and I did many different activities together. We went to the park and museums. We took walks along the lake and went fishing in Rockford, Illinois. My mom and dad taught me diverse concepts and allowed me to explore my thoughts and feelings freely. They were kind and patient. Thinking about it, I don't believe I ever heard either of them raise their voice. When I was seven, my little brother Ethan was born. Things were great for the first two years. I enjoyed being his big brother. Everyone was happy, especially my parents. Suddenly, my home life changed."

Indigo felt Jonathan becoming sad. She receives a vision of how to comfort Jonathan. She places her hand on his back and rubs his back very softly. Jonathan looks at Indigo, smiles, and nods as if to say thank you. Indigo places her hand back on her lap.

Jonathan continues, his voice trembling with the weight of the memories, "When I was nine, my dad fell ill. He was in and out of the hospital. My mom was overwhelmed trying to care for everyone. Ethan didn't understand what was happening. I think the most challenging part was watching my dad's pain as he wanted to play with Ethan, but he was too tired. Since my mom needed help, his mom moved in with us. Sadly, my dad died when Ethan turned three."

Indigo replies tearfully, "I am so sorry, Jonathan."

Jonathan acknowledges her and continues, "My grandmother helped us until Ethan started kindergarten. However, a year later, my grandmother died. I think she was heartbroken that my father, who was her only son, died. After the deaths of both my father and my grandmother, my mom struggled. She spent most of her time working or sleeping. I was responsible for getting Ethan and me safely to and from school. Essentially, our lives were reduced to getting through the day."

Indigo says, "I am so sorry. The deaths of both your dad and grandmother must have been difficult for you and your family. The changes you endured after his passing and during his illness were heartbreaking. You all could have given up, but you kept trying. That takes a lot of courage…When did your stepfather come into the picture?"

Jonathan tries to suppress his emotions; he looks at Indigo and asks, "Would you like to walk?"

"Sure," she replies.

As they walk, Jonathan says agitatedly, "My stepfather came into our lives my freshman year of high school. There's not much to say. I believe my mom was lonely and connected with my stepfather. He and my mom got married my senior year. We don't talk much because he isn't like my father. He does have a better relationship with Ethan, at least."

He sighs, "Honestly, I think my stepfather has negatively influenced my mom. She is less patient and is more strict. For instance, I fixed breakfast for everyone this morning. It was a surprise. Only Ethan greeted me when he, my mom, and my stepfather walked into the kitchen. My stepfather asked me if I had "cleaned the bathroom or cut the grass." As I brought her a plate of food, my mom said she only wanted turkey bacon. Then she snaps at my brother because he told her she was missing some good food. When I was younger, my mom would have said good morning or thank you. She would not have yelled at my brother."

As they walk through the botanical garden, Indigo smiles, looking at the beautiful flowers. They sit on a bench, and Indigo sees two swans in a pond. The pond has a miniature waterfall. Indigo says, "Oh wow, I haven't seen a waterfall before. Look at those swans. They are perfectly connected."

The swans circle around the pond and float near them. Jonathan sees that the swans are chipped and laughs, "Those swans are fake."

Indigo laughs and places her hand on Jonathan's back, "After that difficult conversation, we needed a laugh.

I am sorry about all you have endured. Thank you for sharing."

Indigo and Jonathan take their time walking through the botanical garden. They stop and look at many of the exhibitions. Jonathan looks across the street and notices a sandwich shop on the corner. He points to the shop and says, "Would you like to get something to eat?"

At that moment, Indigo feels and hears a rumble in her stomach and responds, "That would be nice."

Jonathan and Indigo cross the street and enter the sandwich shop. They look over the menu. Indigo tells Jonathan she is a vegetarian. They both order two small veggie subs and two glasses of water. They wait patiently for their food. Indigo insists on paying. The cashier calls their name, and they pick up their trays at the counter. They walk to a booth in the corner and sit down.

Jonathan says, "Indigo, I really shouldn't complain. My friend Darius has it much harder than I do. His father was never around; he has three brothers and a sister. They live in a tiny apartment, and they have roaches. His family is on public assistance, and his sister, who is only 16, has a baby. His oldest brother is in and out of jail. His two younger brothers are both in a gang."

Indigo interrupts, "Jonathan, I have no desire to sound mean. I think comparing yourself to others is not a good idea. Doing that is a distraction from your life. I forgot to ask you if you had talked with anyone to deal with your loss?"

Jonathan reflects, "You are right Indigo. I apologize. Thank you for interjecting. The issue was my family life, and I focused on my friend. They provided a counselor in high school, and I attended a support group. Talking to you was the first time I opened up about my dad outside of the group."

"Oh, before I forget," Indigo pulls a journal from her backpack. "Jonathan, I picked this up for you. Every night, write about your day and your thoughts. Every morning, write about your intentions."

"Thank you for thinking of me and getting me a journal," Jonathan says. He takes a moment, then responds, "I haven't had anyone randomly get me anything since my dad died."

Indigo and Jonathan finish their meal, disposing of their trash before heading towards the door and exiting the sandwich shop. As they step outside, Indigo inquires, "When is class over for you?"

Jonathan responds, raising his eyebrows, "In one week. Why do you ask?"

"Oh, I saw a wonderful-looking place on my way into Chicago. It's called Pictured Rocks National Lakeshore. I have a friend who will drive us there if I contact her. I can plan the trip for August, two months from now," Indigo suggests enthusiastically.

"I would love to go. I haven't been outside of Chicago since my dad died," Jonathan admits. "Are you sure your friend won't mind taking us?"

"Oh, she won't mind at all. I will call her tonight so she can clear her schedule," Indigo assures him.

"Great! I can't wait," Jonathan exclaims.

Indigo suggests, "Let's meet up tomorrow."

"That would be great," Jonathan says eagerly.

Jonathan extends his arms for a hug, surprising Indigo. She awkwardly reciprocates, sharing a brief, heartfelt hug. After their embrace, Indigo walks away, and Jonathan waits for his Uber.

Jonathan arrives home and finds his younger brother immersed in a video game. Jonathan picks up the other controller and joins him. The two siblings spend the next three hours bonding over video games. After the last match, Jonathan goes to his room and thinks about his day with Indigo. He takes off his shoes and places them in the closet. Jonathan sits on the bed with his back against the headboard and opens the journal Indigo gave him. He takes a deep breath and begins to write.

Indigo arrives at the alley. She glances around cautiously before manifesting her crystal pod and entering. She settles into her chair and retrieves the journal from her backpack. Thoughts of the day with Jonathan weigh on her mind, especially his challenging home situation. Later that night, Indigo telepathically plans the trip to Pictured Rocks National Lakeshore.

She makes telepathic contact with Bríg, a being from the fourth dimension. "Bríg, I have an unusual request. I've planned a camping trip in this third dimension with my friend Jonathan. I need your assistance with driving us there," Indigo says.

Bríg excitedly says, "Really? Camping in the third dimension? I'd be happy to drive!"

"Thank you so much Bríg. I really appreciate your help."

"You know we are neighbors and try to assist one another no matter what dimension we are from," Bríg smiles.

Indigo asks, "Can you tell me more about the fourth dimension?"

"Oh, Indigo. I am sure the fourth doesn't look like the fifth. However, we aren't as dense as the third. We see time as malleable. We can observe past and future events simultaneously. Space in my world is like a tapestry woven tight with unseen threads, connecting every possibility. Imagine walking into a room in the third dimension, Indigo. You see the walls, the floor, the ceiling, right? But in the fourth, you'd also see the echoes of that room. You would see the past versions, future iterations, all layered on top of each other," Bríg smiles.

Indigo enthusiastically says, "Your dimension sounds amazing. Thank you for sharing and thank you for agreeing to take us camping. I can't wait to go as I think this trip will help him. The trip will be on August 2nd. I will remind you the day before as I am adjusting to the concept of time."

Bríg responds, "Indigo, I can't wait to go…I will see you then."

The following day, Jonathan calls Indigo. He asks her to meet him at the coffee shop in 30 minutes. Indigo heads to the coffee shop. When she arrives, she orders a cup of coffee for Jonathan and water for herself. As she waits, she reflects on their time together.

Jonathan arrives at the coffee shop and sits down across from Indigo. He says gratefully, "Thank you for the coffee. I enjoyed our day at the botanical gardens yesterday."

Indigo replies with a warm smile, "I enjoyed it too."

Jonathan sighs, sharing, "In that short time, I forgot about the harshness of the city. All I had to do was step into the botanical garden and connect with nature."

Indigo empathizes, "I can't fully grasp the harshness of this city, but I'm beginning to see it through your eyes."

Jonathan suggests, "How about we ride around Chicago on the train? It'll help you understand the battles I face daily."

Nervously, Indigo agrees, "Yes, I think it would help me. My exposure has been limited."

Jonathan advises, "Just be prepared. You must stay aware when we're walking and on the train."

They head to the train station. Along the way, Indigo appears carefree. Jonathan observing her warns, "If you keep looking so carefree, you might draw attention to yourself."

Arriving at the train station, Indigo feels overwhelmed by the crowd. The train arrives and they board. As the train gets packed, Indigo is pushed, stumbling into Jonathan. As they ride through the city, Indigo reaches for her backpack, but Jonathan stops her. In a calm tone, he reminds her, "Don't draw attention. It's not always safe here."

Indigo acknowledges the harsh reality. She whispers, "I felt overwhelmed when I first arrived, but now, seeing more of the city, I can better grasp your struggles. The areas are filled with abandoned buildings and so many homeless people."

Jonathan says, "This is why opening up about my home life was difficult. You need to act tough not to attract attention. That is probably why I deflected attention onto my friend. Living in this environment forces you to hide and lose touch with yourself." Jonathan realizes he should be close to his neighborhood. He looks out the window, "Let me show you where I live."

They disembark the train and head towards Jonathan's neighborhood, where the atmosphere changes. Indigo observes, "The weather has shifted."

Jonathan nods, admitting, "This isn't the best neighborhood."

He points out his house. Indigo is overwhelmed by the sights and surroundings. She thinks, *my journal reflection from the first day holds. I sense that people in this dimension have lost hope.*

They take an Uber back to the coffee shop, Jonathan shares, "I could easily take the train or walk since I'm only three miles away. But sometimes, I take this short car ride to tune out the city. It helps, even if it's brief."

Indigo says, "I might not fully grasp it, but I realize why you would do things to escape temporarily."

Indigo receives insight on supporting Jonathan and suggests, "Let's meet tomorrow to work on a vision board. It won't help you escape, but it'll give you something positive to focus on."

Jonathan agrees, "I've never done a vision board before, but tomorrow sounds good."

He hugs Indigo before walking home. Indigo heads to the alley and makes her crystal pod appear. As she enters her pod, she reflects on the train ride through the city.

Indigo writes in her journal. "As my inner guide said, I am seeing firsthand the difficulties and trials within this dimension." She sighs, continuing to write:

"So many faces were all around,

Yet I felt alone walking the streets.

I saw empty lives,

Lost to what society had sown into them.

They are merely going through the motions of life,

Living it as an empty routine.

Instead of realizing their lives are unfulfilled,

They stuff themselves with temporary fulfillments.

They fail to realize this comes at a cost,

For, in the end, their inner light has faded away."

Indigo closes her journal, tears streaming down her cheeks. She realizes her inner light is dimming. Her thoughts drift to her mother's similar experience. Indigo reaches within, connecting with her inner guide, finding comfort and peace.

Chapter 3

The next day, Indigo's phone rings. "Would you like to get something to eat at the coffee shop in an hour?" Jonathan asks.

Indigo replies excitedly, "Yes, I would like to. Remember, we are working on our vision boards afterward."

They hang up, and Indigo thinks, "I have never made a vision board. Hmmm, I wonder what I will need."

Indigo receives a flash of information. She envisions two blank poster boards, tape, and four magazines that appear quickly. She places the items in her backpack and walks to the coffee shop. Indigo and Jonathan arrive at the same time. They order vegetarian sandwiches. Indigo orders water, and Jonathan orders a hot, vanilla-flavored coffee. They sit at the table by the cafe's window.

Their names are called, and they walk to the counter to get their food. They walk back to the table. Indigo asks Jonathan if she can taste his coffee. Jonathan gives her the cup. Indigo takes a sip, sputters, and gasps, "Why do you drink this?!"

Jonathan chuckles and says, "I should have warned you, as the taste is a little intense. I drink coffee as a way to ease some of my anxiety."

They take time to eat and enjoy their sandwich. They look around the shop. After eating, they place their sandwich basket near the trash and walk to the park.

Jonathan says, "That was nice to eat our lunch in silence. I felt very relaxed and probably didn't need the coffee. I am so used to having conversations when I eat."

Indigo receives a flash, "It is called mindful eating. Mindful eating helps to get in tune with the senses by becoming more aware and decreasing anxiety."

Jonathan smiles, "I am always learning something new when we are together."

They arrive at the park bench, and Indigo pulls the supplies out of her backpack and places them on the table. As she is about to close her backpack, Jonathan sees her notebook.

Jonathan asks, "Is that your journal?"

Indigo replies, "Yes. Last night I wrote a poem I would like you to read. After spending the day riding through the city, I felt overwhelmed."

"I know journals are personal. I appreciate that you are willing to share it with me," Jonathan responds.

Indigo shows Jonathan her journal.

Jonathan reads the poem and asks, "Can you explain it?"

Indigo takes a deep breath, "This is how I felt yesterday. Remember I told you that we encourage each other in Serenity Haven? There is an aura that exists within that is visible to everyone."

Jonathan's eyebrows raise, "What's an aura?"

Indigo continues, "Your aura is the light that shines from within. It is a clear representation of your consciousness. It consists of your emotional and spiritual state. The poem was about how I didn't see the light within others yesterday. Although people were all around me, I felt alone. People seemed disconnected and empty. I felt that the streets were graveyards of dreams and unmet goals, where people were merely going through life. People face the temptation to conform to a life that is not real simply because that is what people are born into. To escape, people often attempt to fill their lives with relationships, material possessions, or various beliefs. But I believe that people can rediscover themselves. If people can discover their inner light, they will find the journey worthwhile."

Jonathan pauses for a moment, "Wow, that is amazing, Indigo. You see things with great clarity for not being from this environment. I have never known anyone in touch with who they are."

Indigo smiles, "Let's work on the vision boards. You will find words or pictures in the magazines, cut them out, and place them on your vision board with the tape. There is no right or wrong way to do this. The main point is that you are trying to envision your current goals and your future. While doing the vision board, we can talk about each word. By talking about the words, we are making them come alive."

Jonathan says, "I thought about what happened when we were eating yesterday. You asked me about my life, and I started telling you about my friend's life. I have been taking psychology classes with no real goal. I realize I would like to help younger teenagers break the chains of poverty which I learned can take four generations to break. I wrote this down in my journal last night as you said we would be working on vision boards today. I detailed all the concepts needed to end the cycle."

Indigo smiles, "It is good you recognize talking about someone else's issues doesn't help you. In what you stated, you realize it isn't your friend's fault regarding the cycles. I am happy you are willing to do something about the issue."

Indigo grabs a magazine and finds the word light. She cuts it out and says, "I would like to present my best self to others. I want the world to see a beautiful light within me; as we all should reflect a greater light."

Jonathan replies, "Wow, that was nicely said. It correlates to the message you wrote in your journal. Jonathan finds a picture of a dollar. He cuts it out and says, "The reason I am choosing money is so that I can learn how to manage money wisely and to teach others. One of the issues is that we all have wants, but we don't understand that wants are not our needs. If we can choose wisely and save, we can eventually get more than our needs met. Also, teaching financial skills is important in breaking the cycle of poverty."

Indigo replies, "That is good for understanding the difference between needs and wants."

Jonathan sees the word gratification. He reflects, "I am guilty of trying to do things that will instantly "satisfy" me. I want to teach young people that we shouldn't focus on instant gratification."

"Yes, I agree with you about instant gratification. Hmmm, I think we should take a break and walk around the park," Indigo senses something important will occur.

"That's a good idea," Jonathan responds.

They stand, gathering their belongings. Walking through the park, they see a figure hunched over on the grass, which catches their eye. An older man with worn clothes is amidst a clutter of objects. He motions for them. As they approach him, he says, "You two," his voice hoarse, "I have seen you there, fiddlin' with paper and pictures. What's that all about?"

Jonathan hesitates, unsure how to explain. Indigo responds, "We're making vision boards. Mapping out our hopes and dreams for the future."

The man replies with bitterness etched into his face, "Dreams, huh?" He scoffs and chuckles, "Had plenty of those once. I had big ones. But life, it chews 'em up and spits 'em out. Now I got nothin' left but this patch of dirt and these scraps," he gestures to the jumble of belongings.

Silence hangs heavy in the air. Jonathan feels empathy, the echo of his past struggles resonating with the man's despair.

Indigo looks down on the ground, "I am sorry that life has treated you this way."

Jonathan agrees with Indigo. Jonathan hesitantly touches the man on his shoulder. The man acknowledges the gesture.

Jonathan and Indigo walk away from the man. Jonathan feels heavy after the conversation. Indigo says, "Let's sit by the water. I have my blanket in my backpack."

Indigo and Jonathan find a spot near the lake and lie on the blanket. They are both looking up at the sky. Jonathan says in despair, "I told you that people are struggling. Do you know how many people feel like he does? I wish there was more that I could do. What could I have said that would make a difference?"

Indigo sighs and tearfully says, "I share your wish for us to do more to help him. But that is why we are working on the vision board. Perhaps there's another person out there whom you can help."

"You are right. Just give me a moment to look at the sky," Jonathan replies. He looks up at the sky for another ten minutes. He stands up, "Okay, I need to finish my vision board."

Indigo folds her blanket and puts it back in her backpack. They return to the park bench and continue working on the vision board.

Jonathan cuts out the word education. He tapes the word onto the board, "My goal is to graduate from college."

Jonathan cuts out the words job and skills. He says, "It is important for others to have the right skills for the employment they seek."

Jonathan gets excited at seeing the word entrepreneurship, "My goal is to take everything I have learned and open a teen center. I would like the center to be a haven for teens after school and during the summer. I would like to take teenagers on field trips. I think it is important to get people out of their environment."

Indigo says, "That is a nice goal of providing a haven to others."

Jonathan finds another word: financial freedom. "I wish there weren't so many obstacles to getting things started." He looks down at the ground.

Indigo receives a vision, "While at school, write up every aspect of your plan. Use that time to connect with agencies that could help you."

"Yes, you are right," Jonathan replies. He finds two words and places them on the top of his board. They are generational changes.

Indigo says, "Oh, generational changes. That is perfect as it connects to your goals."

Jonathan finds investing. He says, "I would like to have a scholarship fund. Anyone who wants to attend college will be encouraged to apply to the fund."

Jonathan cuts out the word voice. He looks down, "I want to help young people find their voice. Right now, I don't feel I have found mine."

Indigo replies, "You may not feel as though you have found your voice yet, but that is what these exercises are for. It is to help you find and develop your voice."

Jonathan cuts out the word creativity. He proclaims, "I do believe creativity is important. In my first psychology class, I learned that creativity is at the top of the taxonomy for learning. Creative thinkers can think out of the box and put many ideas together. I want to teach teenagers how to use this to express themselves positively and to help others."

Jonathan excitedly cuts out the next word, critical thinking. He says, "I had an elementary school teacher who taught me the importance of critical thinking. Your way of being reminds me of the importance of critical thinking. You are very mindful in your approach to life. You have a way of internally questioning and processing. Critical thinking and creative thinking go hand in hand."

Jonathan finds another word and cuts it out. It is leadership. He states, "Leadership means taking the initiative and inspiring others to make a difference. I believe that leaders should set a positive example."

Indigo stops Jonathan and asks him to reflect briefly on the words on his vision board.

Jonathan looks at the board. "I would like teenagers to have courage and resilience. Things may not always go as expected, but we must bounce back and try again."

Jonathan looks at Indigo, who only has the word light on her vision board. Indigo sees Jonathan looking at her, "Today, I realized I would like to be a social worker like my mom. She helps people as they move through Serenity Haven to the other islands. I didn't think I wanted to do the same thing. However, after being here in Chicago, I feel that this is what I should be doing when I go back home. That is the reason I only have light on my vision board."

"That's really nice," he says.

As Indigo is talking to Jonathan, her mom is watching from the fifth dimension. She looks at her indigo light and telepathically says, "She is growing from this experience. Her aura is shining brighter."

Jonathan looks at his phone and realizes that it is getting late. He tells Indigo that he needs to go home to be with Ethan before his mom and stepfather go out for the evening. Indigo informs Jonathan that she will walk around the park a little longer to reflect before going home. Jonathan reminds Indigo to be careful and orders an Uber. They hug, and Indigo walks toward the small lake in the park. Jonathan walks towards the main road to wait for his Uber.

When Indigo returns to her pod, she reflects on the vision boards. She writes in her journal:

"As the dreams of teens may seem far away or unattainable,

Remember, hope can be a small flame.

You will face many dark times.

But, remember, every mistake can lead to growth.

Don't wait for situations to change,

But be brave and be the spark of light you want to see in your world.

Because your little light can light up a dark and lonely world!"

Jonathan arrives home. He immediately places his vision board on his wall. Ethan walks into the room and asks Jonathan about the vision board. Jonathan explains to Ethan the meaning of the vision board and what each word means. Jonathan shares his goals with Ethan. Ethan's eyes light up with hope. He asks Jonathan to help him make a vision board.

The next morning, Jonathan calls Indigo and tells her he will spend the day helping Ethan make a vision board. Indigo is very happy that Jonathan is trying to inspire others. Jonathan goes to the store to purchase items for the board and a journal for Ethan. When Jonathan returns home, he sets the board on the kitchen table and calls Ethan into the kitchen. Ethan enters the kitchen, and Jonathan reaches into his backpack and pulls out a journal.

Ethan asks, "What is this?"

Jonathan replies, "This is your journal. I started writing in mine a few days ago. Indigo gave me the journal and taught me that at the end of the day, I should reflect on how the day went. I should reflect honestly and recognize any negative behaviors or actions. In the morning, I write the behavior I am focused on that day in the journal."

Ethan says, "That is a great idea. Thank you for the journal."

Jonathan helps Ethan make his vision board. Ethan cuts out the word hope and places the word on the top of his board.

Ethan rubs his head, "I struggled with not having our dad around. However, I have watched you. Even though we have lost both our dad and grandmother, you are trying hard. You are an inspiration."

When they finish the vision board, Ethan enters his room and hangs it on the wall. Ethan takes time to write in his journal. Jonathan enters his room and writes about helping Ethan with his vision board in his journal. Later, Jonathan and Ethan go downstairs and play video games together.

Meanwhile, Indigo spends the day reflecting. She thinks about Jonathan helping Ethan and writes in her journal. She receives a call from Jonathan.

Indigo says, "Hello."

Jonathan replies, "I have a busy week studying for the exams. But I want you to come over Friday night for dinner. My mom and stepfather will be home, and I would like you to meet them."

Indigo, understanding the importance of his studies, replies reassuringly, "That's fine. I have work that I need to catch up on." She hesitates, "I would like to meet your parents."

In the days leading up to Friday, as Jonathan focuses on his final exams, Indigo uses the time to embrace the park and the coffee shop. Indigo appreciates the moments she is spending in the third dimension. She knows that she will be a light of consciousness once she returns to Serenity Haven.

Friday morning arrives, bringing a sense of anticipation for Jonathan. Jonathan takes his final exams and eagerly returns home. While cleaning the house, he calls Indigo, who is walking in the park. Her phone rings. Jonathan's voice greets her, "You can come by my house at 6 pm. I will make sure you have a vegetarian pizza."

Indigo responds warmly, "Thank you. I will be there."

Concerned about her safety, Jonathan asks, "Do you remember how to get here?"

Indigo pauses briefly before replying confidently, "Yes, I remember how to get there."

Jonathan, being cautious, insists, "Take an Uber since you are still unaware of your surroundings."

Indigo agrees, "I will be safe," before hanging up. However, she couldn't help but smile as she thought, "I don't need an Uber. I plan on envisioning myself at your house."

Indigo returns to her crystal pod, and with her thoughts, she manifests a beautiful bouquet in a vase. Satisfied with the bouquet, she closes her eyes, and when she opens them, she is at Jonathan's house. She knocks on the door.

Jonathan opens the door and briefly scans the street for an Uber, finding none. He shakes his head, hugs Indigo warmly, and invites her inside. As he glances at the bouquet in her hands, he can't help but think, "She is kind."

Jonathan introduces Indigo to his mom and stepfather, who are watching television. Indigo gives Jonathan's mom the flowers.

She says, "Thank you. The vase is unique." But thinks, *This is unusual. Who gives something to someone they don't know?*

Jonathan's stepfather looks at Indigo and thinks, *looks like she's not from around here.*

Indigo asks, "Where is your brother Ethan?"

"He went to his friend's house for the night," Jonathan replies.

Jonathan's mom says, "So, you're Jonathan's friend from the park, right?"

Indigo smiles, "Yes, I am. It's nice to meet you, Mrs. Mitchell."

"Call me Linda," she says. She points to her husband, "That is Scott, my husband."

Scott says, "Yeah, nice to meet you, Indigo." He continues to watch television.

Indigo replies, "Nice to meet you too, Mr. Scott."

Indigo and Jonathan both sit on the couch and watch the news.

Scott points at the TV, "Can you believe all this is happening? The world's gone mad."

Linda says, "Scott, ease up. You know you get overly excited watching the news."

"I'm just saying, Linda. These immigrants are coming in, causing problems," Scott replies.

Indigo uneasily says, "Well, there are always different perspectives on those issues."

"Perspective? It's about protecting our own," Scott scoffs.

The news transitions to a segment on international affairs.

Scott mutters, "And don't get me started on these overseas problems. Always meddling where we shouldn't be."

Indigo anxiously says, "Sometimes, global issues are interconnected, and understanding helps find solutions."

Linda interrupts, "Let's change the subject, shall we? Pizza's here."

They sit around the dining table, eating silently. The atmosphere is tense.

Scott, still upset with the news, says, "Republicans, Democrats—it's all a mess. Can't trust any of them."

Jonathan tries to steer the conversation away from controversial topics.

Jonathan asks, "How's work? Anything new?"

Scott grumbles, "Same old, same old. You know how it is."

Indigo says, "Thank you for dinner. I appreciate your hospitality. I apologize, I need to leave because it is getting late."

Linda replies, "You're welcome. Come back anytime."

Jonathan walks Indigo to the door and talks outside his house. Jonathan says, "First, I apologize for my stepfather's behavior."

Indigo says, "It is fine, Jonathan. You told me about your family when we went to the Botanical Garden. I appreciate you sharing your home life by inviting me to dinner. That means a lot to me."

Jonathan responds, "Also, I want you to know that when I took my psychology exam today, I realized something important. In the vision board I created, I told you I desired to help others break the cycle. I even talked about the importance of critical thinking. I internally felt it was everyone else's issue. I believed they were the ones who were trapped."

Indigo replies, "Yes, Jonathan. I thought you didn't see your issues."

He chuckles in disbelief, "Hilarious, isn't it? My issues blinded me."

Indigo nods in agreement.

Jonathan inhales deeply, "All this knowledge I've accumulated. All these theories and studies were simply decorations for my mind. However, I wasn't confronting my prejudices or questioning my preconceptions."

He puts his head down, "It's like I was reading about another species. I was dissecting their flawed reasoning. I never realized I was pointing the magnifying glass in the wrong direction."

Indigo moves closer, her eyes filled with compassion. She says, "So, the change starts at home, which means within you?"

"Exactly. No more lecturing on critical thinking while I mindlessly accept whatever my conditioning tells me. It's time to put my words into action," Jonathan responds.

Indigo shakes her head in agreement.

Jonathan passionately says, "I have to admit it's terrifying, Indigo. Leaving my comfort zone and exposing the cracks in my foundation."

Indigo touches his back. She says, "This is a big step as it is the start of self-awareness. You are able to self-reflect."

"Thank you, Indigo," Jonathan replies.

"Jonathan, I do need to get home. You know it is getting late, and you don't like me being in certain areas," she says.

Jonathan hugs Indigo. Indigo leaves. As soon as she walks a few doors down, she closes her eyes and returns to her crystal pod. Indigo sighs and feels heavy about the conversation she had with Scott. She thinks about what he said in regards to only his perspective mattering and thinks of the struggles children face when the adults around them aren't open to new ideas or other points of view.

She writes in her journal: "In this short time, I have seen the growth in Jonathan. Initially, he had many theories and ideas of how he would like to solve the issues. However, he lacked internal and external actions. Today, we had a conversation showing he is starting to awaken. He recognizes his lack of self-reflection. Also, he was willing to share information about himself and show his home even though he knows the home dynamics are currently toxic." Indigo closes her journal and slowly falls asleep.

Now that finals are over, Jonathan meets Indigo at the park in the mornings. They take walks and talk. They enjoy laughing and spending time together.

One evening, he calls Indigo and asks if she wants to volunteer at the food pantry on June 29th. Jonathan tells Indigo his brother Ethan will also be volunteering. He tells her the name of the food pantry. When Indigo gets off the phone with Jonathan, she envisions the food pantry's location. Indigo feels tired and decides to rest. She is pleased that Jonathan would like to volunteer. She eagerly anticipates their next adventure.

Chapter 4

It's 4 am on Saturday. Jonathan gets up and brushes his teeth. He changes into his exercise clothes and does morning stretches. He takes a shower and gets dressed. Jonathan settles into his chair and begins to write his intentions for the day: "Today will be a good day. We are volunteering at the food pantry for the first time. I must set a good example because Ethan is coming with us."

Jonathan closes his journal and sits comfortably on the floor with his back against the bed. He takes a deep breath and slowly releases it. Jonathan begins to picture the day. Vivid images of him, Indigo, and Ethan appear in his mind. They smile and enjoy helping and serving others. The day ends with a trip to the smoothie shop and an Uber ride home.

Jonathan slowly opens his eyes and looks at the time on the clock, it's 6:07 am. Jonathan stands up and walks towards Ethan's room. He knocks on Ethan's door and slowly opens it. To his surprise, Ethan is already awake.

"Morning, J.," Ethan says with a glimmer in his eyes. "Ready for the big day?" He asks.

Jonathan replies, "Yes, I am. But I am shocked to see you up and getting dressed."

Ethan smiles, "Of course, I'm up. I get to spend the day with my big brother and finally meet Indigo."

Jonathan laughs, "I'm glad you are looking forward to the day. I'm going downstairs to fix croissants with cheese and some fruits for us. We will leave around 7 am. We are meeting Indigo at Mana Food Pantry at 8 am."

Jonathan backs out of Ethan's room, slowly closing the door behind him. He goes downstairs into the kitchen to prepare breakfast. He takes out his phone and plays "calm music" on YouTube. Jonathan peels and slices a mango. He washes and cuts the strawberries into halves. He makes croissants with butter and gets the cheese cubes from the refrigerator. Jonathan divides the food evenly between two plates and places the food on the table. He goes into the pantry and gets two bottles of water. He places one bottle next to each plate on the table. Ethan walks into the kitchen. They take their seats and prepare to eat.

"Thanks, J.," Ethans says.

Jonathan nods and smiles as the two of them eat their food. Once they finish, Ethan quickly grabs both plates. He washes the plates as Jonathan cleans the table. They go outside, sit on the porch, and wait for their Uber.

Ethan says, "Jonathan, you should use some of the money you saved from working to buy a car."

"Maybe one day. I'm just trying to get myself going in the right direction. I'm afraid the freedom of a car may become more of a distraction than I can manage," Jonathan replies.

"A distraction?" Ethan inquires.

"Yes, with increased freedom comes increased responsibility. I know I'm not ready for that. I would likely spend too much time in my car escaping stressful situations. Instead, I want to focus on my goals and work on myself," Jonathan replies.

Ethan looks at Jonathan curiously. The Uber arrives. They walk to the car, verify the driver, get in, and put on their seatbelts.

"I see you are going to Mana Food Pantry. I hear they have a good selection. You guys are picking up food for your family?" The driver asks.

"No, we are going to help volunteer with bagging the food for distribution tomorrow," Ethan says proudly.

"Volunteer!" The driver exclaims, "Man, I ain't volunteering for nothing. Either I am getting paid or it's not happening!"

Ethan looks at Jonathan. Jonathan signals Ethan with his eyes to not respond to the statement. Ethan agrees and begins playing a game on his phone. The driver checks his rearview mirror and notices Ethan on his phone. He looks over at Jonathan, "These youngsters today are so easily distracted. They can't finish a conversation without picking up their phone."

Jonathan doesn't respond to the driver's comments and calmly shifts his gaze out of the window. A few moments later, they arrive at the food pantry. Jonathan tips the driver through the app and says, "Thank you."

He and Ethan exit the car and see Indigo standing outside the food pantry.

"Hi, Jonathan! And this must be Ethan," Indigo says, extending her hand to greet Ethan.

Ethan reaches for Indigo's hand, "Nice to meet you."

Jonathan hugs Indigo, "Good morning. Are you ready for our first adventure?"

"I'm looking forward to it," Indigo replies.

The three of them walk through the door and are warmly greeted.

"Good Morning! Welcome to Mana. How can I help you? My name is Clara," the woman says.

"Good Morning! My name is Indigo. This is Ethan and his brother Jonathan. We are here to volunteer," Indigo pleasantly says while Ethan and Jonathan wave.

"Oh yes, yes," Clara says as she walks toward them. "I hope you don't mind hugs," she says while hugging Indigo, Jonathan, and Ethan.

"Please, follow me," Clara says as she walks towards a room in the back of the building.

They reach a pair of double wooden doors. Clara opens the door on the right and gestures for them to go inside. The room has several long folding tables filled with food and four deep freezers. Two women are setting up long folding tables at the back of the room. The women hear them enter and take a moment to wave and walk towards them.

As they get closer, Clara says pointing to each person, "This is April and Margaret."

April and Margaret both say, "Welcome." They extend their arms and take turns hugging them.

"Clara, I know you have plenty of things to do before we hand out the food tomorrow. We will show these three around and explain what they need to do," Margaret says. April and Margaret guide them toward the paper bags. Clara exits the room.

"Let's start here," says Margaret.

"Ethan, you can start here. Insert one paper bag inside the other until we have 150 double paper bags. You can place the bags here on the floor as you complete them. Also, place a tick mark on this sheet of paper for every ten bags you complete. This way, you don't have to try to track all the bags," Margaret says.

"Yes, ma'am," replies Ethan as he eagerly inserts one paper bag into the other to make the double paper bags.

Margaret points at the tables full of food, "This area is self-explanatory. All you have to do is place the correct item number in each bag. Besides, if you forget, there is a number in front of each item on the table to remind you," Margaret says to Jonathan and Indigo.

Jonathan and Indigo nod to indicate they understand what Margaret has shared about the number in front of each table.

"April, I'll let you explain the process as I fill a bag," Margaret says.

"Very well," responds April.

"First, you guys will each pick up a bag. Then, you will walk down each aisle and place the number of items indicated for that table into the bag. We will follow Margaret as she places each item into the bag. At the end, you will see how each completed bag should look," says April.

Margaret picks up one of the bags Ethan completed and begins walking down the row. She places two cans of beans and a bag of rice in the bag from the first table. Margaret moves down to the next table, and they follow behind her. She places one can of ravioli and soup into the bag. The following table contains canned spaghetti sauce. She places two cans of spaghetti sauce in the bag.

Margaret turns right at the end of the first row. She begins to walk up the next row. April, Indigo, and Jonathan follow her. The first table of the second row contains spaghetti. She places one package of spaghetti in the bag. The following table holds two-pound bags of rice. She places one bag of rice in the bag. The final table in the second row has quart-size ziploc bags of flour. Margaret places one bag of flour into the paper bag. They all turn left and begin walking down the third and final row. The first two tables contained loaves of bread. Margaret places one loaf of bread into the bag. The last table held jars of peanut butter and jars of jelly. Margaret places one jar of each in the bag.

Then she walked over to the empty folding tables that she and April were putting into place when Indigo, Ethan, and Jonathan first entered the room. April, Indigo, and Jonathan follow her. She places the completed bag at the far edge of the very first table.

Margaret faces Indigo and Jonathan and says, "That's it. Easy peasy."

Indigo and Jonathan look at each other, then at Margaret, and Jonathan says, "Ok, I believe we've got it. Thank you for taking your time and showing us exactly what to do."

"Yes. Thank you," Indigo added.

"Ok. We have other tasks if you guys are okay with working alone?" Margaret asks.

"Oh yes, we will be just fine," Indigo replies.

April and Margaret walk towards a side door. Margaret says, "We will be in the storage shed if you have any questions." Margaret and April walk out of the building.

Indigo and Jonathan walk towards the front of the room, where Ethan has already completed stacking his third group of ten paper bags.

"Wow! Little brother, you are doing a great job! Keep it up," says Jonathan.

Ethan smiles. He is pleased that Jonathan is happy with his work. Indigo rubs Jonathan's arm. He looks at her, and he can tell she is pleased. Jonathan and Indigo each grab one of the completed paper bags and begin filling the bags as instructed.

About an hour later, Clara decides to see how they are doing. She opens the door. They are working so diligently that neither Jonathan, Indigo, nor Ethan hear her enter the room. She picks up the clipboard, which holds the piece of paper on which Ethan has placed his tick marks. She begins to count.

"Great job, Ethan," Clara says.

Half startled, Ethan quickly turns toward Clara and replies, "Thank you."

"You've finished 140 bags already. That is truly amazing," Clara says with a huge smile.

Jonathan and Indigo hear Clara speaking to Ethan. They put the bags they were holding onto one of the completed bag tables and quickly walked toward Ethan and Clara.

Ethan places the completed paper bag he was holding in its group on the floor. Clara places a big tick mark on the paper, "140 bags indeed, Mr. Ethan. Thank you so much for working so hard and diligently today."

"You are welcome," Ethan says. Ethan is barely able to contain his joy.

Jonathan and Indigo both give Ethan a high five. Jonathan looks at the groups of bags on the floor that need to be filled. He counts four groups of ten. He is surprised that he and Indigo have already filled 100 bags. At that moment, April and Margaret return.

As they get near the other end of the room, Clara says, "These wonderful young people have already filled 100 bags, and Ethan has put together 140 bags," she says while rubbing Ethan's shoulder. Ethan places the bags he is holding on the floor.

As the bag hits the floor, Ethan says, "144."

Everyone begins to clap. Clara, April, and Margaret give Ethan a big group hug. Jonathan and Indigo each grabbed two paper bags off the table and put them together. They release the group hug and notice what Jonathan and Indigo are doing. Clara, Margaret, and April begin to laugh and smile as they each pick up two bags and put them together. Ethan grabs two bags also.
The six of them work together, filling the last 50 bags. It takes about 20 minutes to complete.

Clara says, "On the count of three. Ready 1-2-3!" Everyone places their bag into the final group and shouts, "150!" They all hugged and laughed.

When they are finished, Clara asks, "Would you like some water?"

"That would be nice. Thank you," says Indigo.

Clara starts walking towards the front room. Everyone else follows behind. They reach the front area by the main entrance. Clara hands each person a bottle of water. They each open their bottle and drink the water.

"Thank you, all so much. We really appreciate your help," Clara says. April and Margaret smile in agreement.

Jonathan states, "I would like to thank you for allowing us to help today."

"Yes, thank you," Indigo and Ethan chime in.

The group begins to walk towards the front door. As they reach the door, Clara opens it, "You are welcome back anytime."

They all share hugs and smiles. Ethan, Jonathan, and Indigo leave the food pantry. Their Uber arrives and takes them to Giordano's Pizza. They exit the Uber and enter Giordano's.

Indigo says, "I will pay for the pizza."

"That is very kind of you. Thank you!" Ethan replies.

Jonathan adds, "Yes. Thank you."

The greeter escorts them to their booth. "Your waiter will be with you shortly." He hands them three menus and departs.

Sometime later, the waiter arrives. They order a medium deep-dish spinach pizza and three lemonades. They talk until the pizza arrives. Jonathan says, "Today I learned the importance of helping others without wanting anything in return." Ethan and Indigo agree.

The lemonade and pizza arrive. Indigo takes a sip of her lemonade and takes a bite of her pizza, "This is amazing. Thank you for bringing me here."

Ethan says to Indigo, "Thank you for encouraging us to volunteer."

"Yes, thank you! We will never forget this experience. We look forward to doing it again," Jonathan replies.

They spend the next few hours eating, laughing, and talking. After eating, Jonathan orders an Uber. When the car arrives, Indigo tells Ethan and Jonathan she will walk for a while and then go home.

Jonathan and Ethan get into the Uber. The Uber arrives at their home. Ethan jumps out of the car and runs upstairs to his room. Jonathan pays for the Uber and slowly walks towards the house. When he reaches the top step, he turns and looks at the sky. Jonathan thinks about how his life has changed since meeting Indigo. He smiles, walks into the house, and closes the door behind him.

At that moment, Ethan walks downstairs. He goes up to Jonathan and gives him a big hug. Ethan pulls out a 20-dollar bill, "Here J., I want to help pay for the Ubers. You and Indigo taught me a lot today about sharing your resources with others. You didn't have to take me with you, but you did. Giving you money to help pay for the Ubers is my way of showing that I appreciate it."

Jonathan hugs Ethan and says, "Anytime." They walk to the couch and sit down. Jonathan turns on the video game.

The two play video games for the next two hours. Afterward, Jonathan goes upstairs to shower and write in his journal. As he thinks about his morning visualization, he realizes some things didn't happen as planned. He accepts that not everything is going to happen exactly as he visualizes. But regardless, it was a good day.

Indigo completes her walk around the park. She closes her eyes and appears in the alley. She manifests her pod, goes inside, and sits on the floor. Indigo takes a deep breath and pulls out her journal. She thinks about the day.

She writes: "In the shared volunteering space, we discover the power of community. It wasn't just about the cans and bags; it was about the connection forged between hearts. In volunteering, we found a mirror reflecting the beauty of human interconnectedness. Volunteering brings togetherness and responsibility. One of the missing elements in this dimension is that in giving we receive."

Indigo closes her journal and goes to sleep.

The next day, Jonathan meets Indigo at the park. He sees her standing near the water. He walks up to her and says, "I really enjoyed the experience at the food pantry."

Indigo agrees, "Well, it's hot out here. What if we hand out cold water in the park? People could use a little relief."

"Great idea! Let's grab some water bottles, and we can put up a sign offering free water," Jonathan says excitedly.

Jonathan and Indigo go to the store and pick up a case of water. They return to the park and place the water on the table.

Jonathan sees a passerby, "Stay cool! We have free cold water!"

An older woman approaches them, "Well, this is a lovely sight. Young folks like you are doing good for the community, especially in this heat. It warms my heart."

Jonathan replies, "Thank you! It's not much." Jonathan points at Indigo, "She suggested we do something."

"It's appreciated. Sometimes, it feels like the world's forgotten the simple acts of kindness. You're making a difference," the woman responds.

Jonathan and Indigo pass out all the water they bought. They decide to end the day early. Indigo returns to her pod and Jonathan goes home.

Later that evening, Jonathan sees his stepfather sitting on the couch. He asks, "Can we talk?"

Scott replies, "Talk? Fine, what is it now?"

"I can't keep pretending everything's okay," Jonathan says.

Scott impatiently responds, "Spit it out then."

"I've been trying to understand why you are the way you are. You came into my life, and I know nothing about you. When Indigo had dinner with us, you stated your perspective is what matters," Jonathan responds.

Scott replies, "It's true. My perspective is what matters to me. Scott crosses his arms and says, "What, now you some psychologist? You take one class, and you want to psychoanalyze me."

Jonathan replies, "No, I just want to understand. Where does all this skepticism come from? Why can't you see beyond your views? I just want to know about your life."

Scott sighs, "You want to know about my upbringing, huh?"

Jonathan, "Maybe it'll help me understand."

"Fine, you want the truth? I grew up in a rough neighborhood. No silver spoons, no safety nets. I was in and out of foster homes and group homes. I had to fight to survive in those group homes," Scott says, grimacing.

Jonathan is saddened, "I didn't know that."

Scott replies, "I had to be tough to make it through. It's a different world out there, Jonathan. You can't trust everyone. You've got to be skeptical to survive."

Jonathan responds, "I get it was tough, but does it mean you must be so harsh?"

Scott says defiantly, "Harsh times call for harsh measures. Do you think the world cares about you? You've got to make your way."

Jonathan frustratedly says, "Not everyone is out to get you. There's kindness in the world if you just open up."

Scott responds, "Kindness? You have been around that person Indigo too much. I've seen enough of the world to know it's a dog-eat-dog place. People are selfish, and you can't rely on anyone but yourself."

Jonathan frustratedly responds, "Not everything is a battle against the world."

As Jonathan leaves the room, Scott thinks, *maybe he's right that the world isn't a battleground.*

Although Jonathan is upset, he walks into his room and journals. While he is journaling, he realizes that his stepfather's issues stem from not having a stable home, and a wave of compassion overwhelms him. He sends Indigo a text message, "I finally had the courage to talk to my stepfather and now understand his childhood."

After that conversation, Jonathan sees subtle changes within his stepfather. His stepfather tries to find ways to have conversations with him.

As the month of August is quickly approaching, Jonathan, Indigo, and Ethan continue volunteering at the food pantry. Jonathan and Indigo pass out water in the mornings at the park. Jonathan and Indigo are excited about their upcoming camping trip to Pictured Rocks National Lakeshore.

The day before the camping trip, Indigo calls Jonathan, "I am excited about the trip tomorrow. You only need to bring your clothing and personal hygiene. My friend will bring all the food and supplies."

"Oh wow. I appreciate that. I will see you tomorrow," Jonathan says.

They hang up and Indigo rests for the trip.

Chapter 5

It is August 2nd. Jonathan meets Indigo at the park. He has his backpack and is ready for the trip. They sit on the bench and wait for Indigo's friend, Bríg. She drives up in a blue Tesla.

Indigo sees Bríg, "Look, Jonathan, there's Bríg."

Jonathan raises his eyebrows, "That's a nice car. You said you know her from Serenity Haven?"

Indigo replies, "Yes, you can say we are old friends. We live right across dimensionally from each other."

Indigo introduces Jonathan to Bríg. Indigo tells Jonathan to sit in the front with Bríg. As Jonathan sits in the front seat, he asks, "Do you mind if I turn on the radio?"

Bríg replies, "Sure, you can play whatever you want."

Jonathan finds a radio station playing rap. Indigo sighs. Jonathan isn't paying attention and starts to sing. After the song ends, Jonathan realizes he is the only person enjoying the music. Jonathan forgot Indigo doesn't listen to music. He sighs and turns off the radio.

Three hours later, Jonathan had time to think. Indigo hasn't said anything to Jonathan since he turned off the music. Jonathan tells Indigo and Bríg, "I would like to apologize to you both for my behavior earlier. I was so excited about this trip that I made it about myself. Indigo, I know you try to be mindful. Since meeting you, I have been trying to be more aware of the songs I listen to. But now I realize some songs are offensive or don't have a positive message. I wouldn't want younger people to view others as described in many of these songs. I now understand the reason why I should be mindful."

Indigo smiles and says, "Thank you, Jonathan."

Bríg pulls over at a rest area. They exit the vehicle to use the restrooms. When they return to the car, Jonathan looks out the window as he can see the water in the distance.

They arrive at a campsite that is next to the lake.

Bríg sets up their campsite by tossing out the sleeping bags and starting a fire. Jonathan helps Indigo grab the coolers with the food and their backpacks. After unpacking, they sit around the fire. Indigo boils water for their hot chocolate.

Perched on logs around the stone fire ring, they listen to the crackling of the logs, watch the flames dance in a golden glow, and see sparks float toward the sky like flickering stars. Bríg asks Jonathan, "What do you think so far?"

Jonathan replies, "It's not bad. This is my first time camping. I actually kind of like the quiet."

Bríg replies, "Nature has a way of calming the soul. But the real fun begins tomorrow. We will do different trust games."

Jonathan warily asks, "Trust games? What kind of trust games?"

Bríg responds, "Don't worry, nothing too scary. Just some exercises to help you connect. Like the blindfolded walk! Anyway, you two, it's time to rest. We had a long drive."

They each lay inside their sleeping bags. Jonathan pulls out his journal and draws a picture. He closes his journal and looks up at the stars. He smiles and closes his eyes.

The following day, Indigo wakes up and writes in her journal. An hour later, Jonathan rolls over and sees Indigo stretching in front of the lake. Meanwhile, Bríg is making pancakes for them on a little burner. Jonathan gets up and does his hygiene in a nearby area with bushes.

Bríg says, "Okay, you two, breakfast is ready."

Bríg hands Jonathan and Indigo a plate with pancakes and sliced fruit. They sit around, eating and enjoying the morning air. After they finish eating, Indigo cleans up the area.

Bríg says, "Alright, it's time for our first game. It is Truth or Dare. Okay, Jonathan, Truth or Dare?"

"Dare," Jonathan replies.

Bríg says, "Hmm... I dare you to show us the picture you drew last night. When we got into our sleeping bags, I looked over, and you were drawing something."

Jonathan's cheeks flush. He glances at Indigo, whose eyes are filled with encouragement. "Okay, okay, but don't laugh. I'm not exactly Picasso."

He rummages through his backpack and pulls out his journal. He reveals a sketch: a boy standing on a cliff overlooking a vast, star-filled sky.

Bríg's eyes widened, "Wow, Jonathan. Your drawing is beautiful. It feels so real."

Indigo says, "I agree, Jonathan. It's like you poured your heart into this page. What is this boy seeing?"

Jonathan hesitates but responds, "He's seeing possibilities. Underneath the boy is a quote from the Oracle of Delphi. "Know Thyself."

Bríg smiles at Indigo and says, "A drawer and a writer, huh? I knew it! Were you always artistic?"

"I used to draw and write when I was little. But life happened. Many things in my life changed after my father died. I lost my voice," Jonathan replies.

Indigo says, "Look at your drawing. You just needed to find your way back."

Jonathan's eyes sparkle with hope.

Indigo says, "Okay, I have the next trust game." Indigo reaches into her backpack and pulls out a bandana. She says, "I am going to tie this around your eyes. Before you awoke, I took a walk down a trail. I would like to take you on this trail. But you will have to trust me as your guide."

Jonathan hesitantly replies, "Alright. We all remember that I am new to the concept of trust."

Indigo covers Jonathan's eyes. Indigo leads Jonathan down a path. Jonathan stumbles. He almost falls over a rock. He catches his balance, laughing breathlessly. With her hand steady on his back, Indigo gently guides him to a secluded cove with turquoise waves.

Indigo says, "Imagine your fears and burdens that weigh you down. Feel them in your body and your mind. Slowly, let them go. Release them to the wind."

Jonathan breathes deeply. He loosens his body and releases the tension in his jaw. Indigo takes the blindfold off Jonathan's eyes.

Jonathan smiles, "This...this is incredible. It's like another world. I feel so light and clear."

Indigo and Jonathan walk back down the path to the campsite. This time, Jonathan blindfolds Indigo and takes her down the path. Indigo pretends to trip so that Jonathan can catch her. Indigo and Jonathan laugh and return to the campsite.

Jonathan sits on his sleeping bag and opens his backpack. He pulls out a miniature cooler, and inside is a bag with spaghetti noodles and another bag with spaghetti sauce. He says, "I made this for us yesterday morning."

Bríg and Indigo smile. They put their food in bowls and find a spot to sit near the water. As they finish eating, the water reaches Indigo's feet. They get up and place their trash near their camp. Bríg and Jonathan watch as Indigo spontaneously runs into the water.

Indigo shouts, "We might as well enjoy this while we are here."

Jonathan and Bríg join Indigo in the water. They splash and throw water at each other. Afterward, they walk back to the site and change their clothes. They are lying on their sleeping bags.

Bríg says, "Alright, are you all ready for another game?"

She unveils a canvas bag overflowing with mysterious shapes and textures, tied shut with a red bandana.

Jonathan raises his eyebrows, "Bríg, what did you drag out of the woods? Is that a porcupine you plan on making us identify blindfolded?"

Bríg laughs, "Have faith in my culinary adventures! This, my friends, is the Mystery Munch Challenge! Prepare to face the ultimate test of your taste buds!"

Indigo's eyes sparkle with excitement, "Alright, Bríg. We're not afraid of a few mystery nibbles."

"Excellent! The rules are simple. You will take turns reaching inside the bag blindfolded. Using only your taste buds, you need to identify the mystery morsel. One guess per round, fastest" Bríg says.

Bríg places the blindfold on Indigo. Indigo reaches into the bag, her fingers meeting something soft and slightly crumbly. She gingerly pops it in her mouth.

Indigo says, "Hmm, earthy... sweet... almost nutty? Could it be a date?"

"A date? In this bag of wilderness surprises? Bold guess, Indy," Jonathan laughs.

Bríg takes the blindfold off Indigo. Indigo looks in her palm, and there is a plump fig.

Indigo snickers, "See, my wilderness wisdom needs some fine-tuning!"

The game presses on. With each blindfolded encounter, the air is filled with laughter and moments of genuine surprise. A ripe peach is mistaken for an apricot, a plump plum is confused for a nectarine, and a crunchy celery stick is briefly thought to be a slender green bean.

When they finish the game, it is now evening. Jonathan decides he will start the fire. Jonathan grabs a few sticks and attempts to make a fire. Indigo sees Jonathan struggling and says, "Here, let me help you."

Indigo takes the sticks from Jonathan and says, "What's that over there?"

Jonathan looks over in the direction Indigo points to and sees nothing. When he turns his head back, Indigo has started the fire.

Jonathan is confused at how Indigo began the fire so quickly but says nothing. They play another game. This time, it is the storytelling circle.

Bríg says, "Okay, let's play the storytelling game! I'll start, and we will take turns adding to the story. "The sunlight dappled the forest floor as we walked through the woods."

"And a curious squirrel scampered across our path, its bushy tail twitching excitedly," Indigo says.

Jonathan continues, "We were intrigued, so we followed the squirrel deeper into the leafy labyrinth."

"Until we stumbled upon a hidden clearing bathed in emerald light," Bríg says.

Indigo replies, "In the center stood a towering oak, its branches draped in moss and adorned with…"

"Strange, glowing fruit," Jonathan says.

Bríg continues, "Driven by an unknown force, we reach for the fruit. Its touch sends a tingling energy through our fingertips."

"Suddenly, the clearing around us began to twist and distort," Indigo adds, "Morphing into…"

"A fantastical landscape that revealed a waterfall," replies Jonathan.

The three laugh about the story.

Indigo says, "Well, I think I will lie down."

Bríg and Jonathan agree. Jonathan pulls out his journal and reflects on his day. He closes his journal, looks up at the stars with gratitude, and then turns over in his sleeping bag.

The following morning, they wake up and do their personal hygiene. Jonathan has granola bars for them to eat. After eating the granola bars, Jonathan walks over to the water and puts his hand in it. He walks back over to Bríg and Indigo and says, "The games yesterday were about trust and going beyond my five senses. I have learned to trust again and realized I don't need to limit myself by relying on only my physical senses."

Jonathan pauses and looks down at the ground, "I need to be honest about the music incident. The reason I was upset about the music was because my stepfather doesn't like when I play music. Therefore, I immediately reacted defensively. I have definitely been trying harder to be less reactive. Once again, I apologize."

Indigo says, "Jonathan, it takes strength and courage to be vulnerable. The most important thing is you were able to reflect and to admit to your mistake. When you counsel others, this will be important. Anyway, what will your first book be about?"

"It will be about a lost and afraid boy. He learns to hope, believe, and dream beyond the city walls. He eventually finds his voice," Jonathan responds.

Indigo says, "Remember when I told you while working on the vision board that you will need all these activities? Your voice was merely hidden. However, I see you have finally found your voice. It's right here in your actions and your words. You just had to find your way back to it."

They do a group hug. They take their time, pack the car, and return to Chicago. On the ride back to Chicago, Bríg wants to play another game. Bríg says, "Bingo! I spotted a "B" for Bríg! Big billboard advertising Bob's Best Burgers, Bigger Than Your Dreams!"

Jonathan chuckles, "Oh, come on, Bríg, that's a stretch. Your dreams couldn't fit on a whole billboard."

Indigo says, "Look! There's an "E" for Eagle. Eagles soaring above the cornfields!"

"I don't think the eagles would fly above the cornfields, Indigo," Jonathan laughs.

Immediately after, an eagle mysteriously flies over their car. Jonathan sees the eagle and looks around.

Jonathan shakes his head in disbelief then says, "Got one! "I" for Ice cream! That roadside stand has ice cream."

Indigo laughs, "I don't think we will see a roadside stand with ice cream on the highway, Jonathan."

Jonathan thinks *anything is possible. I saw an eagle flying over the car.*

Bríg says, "Alright, now it's time for a round of Highway Haiku! Capture the soul of the road in seventeen syllables. I will go first.

> Sunrise paints the road;
> Trucks hum a highway lullaby,
> Dreams chase distant hills."

Jonathan replies, "That is vivid, Bríg." Jonathan looks around and sees fields with corn and says,

> "Rustled corn whispers;
> Secrets shared in rustling wind,
> Summer sun's warm kiss."

Indigo chimes in,

> "Gravel crunches slowly;
> The winding road a story unfolds,
> Footprints mark the way."

Bríg says,

> "Laughter dances free;
>
> Echoes bounce in mountain air,
>
> Hearts lighter than clouds."

Jonathan replies,

> "Memories like smoke;
>
> Curl and fade in time's cold wind,
>
> Only embers glow."

Indigo says,

> "Future whispers soft;
>
> Paths diverge in fading light,
>
> One step, then another."

"Indigo, those were perfect words for this camping trip," Jonathan says.

The rest of the car ride is quiet. Jonathan reflects on the camping trip. As they get closer to his house, Jonathan thanks Bríg and Indigo for taking him camping. They arrive at his house and he grabs his backpack and calmly walks up the stairs. He looks back and waves as he enters the house. Bríg and Indigo smile and wave back at Jonathan.

Bríg drops Indigo off at the alley. Indigo thanks her and waits for Bríg to leave. She looks around and makes her crystal pod appear. Indigo sits on her blanket and writes in her journal, "I believe this camping trip gave Jonathan the last bit of help he needed." Indigo smiles and reflects on the time of knowing Jonathan. There is a flash, and she realizes she should write a message for Jonathan. She sees that he will understand the messages once she leaves. Indigo tears out papers from her journal and writes:

"Dear Jonathan,

I wanted to share some insights from our time together, along with guidance for when you open your center. Think of your mind as a locked treasure chest filled with answers and dreams. The key to unlocking it resides within you. Here's how:

1. Embrace Humility: To gain knowledge, let go of your ego. Like a bird shedding feathers, you must be open to learning and submit to something greater.

2. Release the Past: Holding onto negative emotions can block your path. Account for your actions, learn from them, and then let go.

3. Create Space for Growth: Just as a garden needs room to flourish, simplify your life by clearing clutter, including people who hinder your progress.
4. Choose Love: Fear and love are the primary emotions that influence our world. Choose love as your guiding force.
5. Be a Light: You can inspire change in others by focusing on tending your own inner light. Remember, self-improvement is a gradual process.
6. Trust Your Intuition: Balance logic with intuition. Clear your mind and open your heart to see the bigger picture.

Remember, a beautiful world awaits you both externally and within. Unlock your heart, let go of what holds you back, and embark on a journey of self-discovery. The treasures you uncover will be priceless."

Indigo folds the paper, places it in her journal, and goes to sleep.

Meanwhile, Jonathan talks to his mom about the camping trip. Jonathan sits at the kitchen table with a cup of hot chocolate. His mom asks, "So, tell me about this camping trip. What did you guys do all weekend?"

Jonathan takes a sip of his hot chocolate, a hesitant smile on his lips.

Jonathan replies, "We hiked, camped, played games...but it was more than that, Mom. It was different."

His mom asks, "Different, how?"

Jonathan replies, "We played trust games. We went on blindfolded walks. The games helped me regain trust. I even showed them a picture I drew."

His mom replies, "Trust games? That sounds interesting."

"It was interesting. At first, I was nervous. I was scared, even. But Indigo and Bríg helped me trust myself," Jonathan replies.

He looks at his mom, his voice filled with a newfound clarity.

"Mom, I realized something on this trip. I realized I'd been closing myself off, shutting out everyone and everything. I was afraid to get hurt again after losing dad," Jonathan says sadly.

His mom reaches across the table and takes his hand.

"Jonathan, I know. I have been at a loss after losing your father. Watching you over the last several months has given me hope. I have noticed the slow changes within you. I saw your and Ethan's vision boards, and am inspired to make one of my own. I was encouraged by you and Ethan's volunteering. I have spoken of helping others when your father was alive, but that dream faded when he died. I would like to volunteer with you and Ethan at least once a month. I have spoken to your stepfather, and we have decided to go to counseling. Somehow, I have noticed little changes within him. Also, I would like to be a better mom to Ethan. I must ensure he has a better environment. Your dad wouldn't have wanted me to be the way I have been," his mom says.

For the first time in many years, Jonathan hugs his mom. She asks if she can see his drawing. Jonathan shows her the drawing and says his goal is to help teenagers find their voice.

His mom's eyes well up with tears, "Jonathan, you will be an amazing counselor."

Jonathan gives his mom another hug, and he goes into his bedroom. He pulls out his journal, writes about the camping trip, and reflects on all he has learned since meeting Indigo. Jonathan smiles, realizing his mom noticed the positive changes. He is happy she will attend counseling so that Ethan can have a chance to find his voice.

Chapter 6

Indigo awakens, embraces the morning sun and does her journaling. As she writes, a sudden flash of realization sweeps over her—the time has come for her to return to Serenity Haven. She takes a deep breath, trying to compose herself, but tears glisten in her eyes as she completes her journal entry. She whispers, "I know I can watch him from afar. But will he remember me?"

With a heavy heart, Indigo makes her way to the park. She reminisces about the countless moments she shared with Jonathan. She thinks, "There were so many times I struggled, but the moments of joy were truly amazing."

At the park, Indigo sits on a familiar bench. She gazes into the water. She doesn't notice Jonathan's approach until he sits beside her.

"What's wrong, Indigo?" Jonathan asks.

Indigo takes a deep breath and replies, "My time here, at this job, has come to an end. I've completed my investigation, and now it's time for me to return to Serenity Haven."

Jonathan's eyes reflect the sorrow in his heart as he listens. He knows that Indigo had initially mentioned that her stay was temporary. However, it doesn't make the farewell any easier. Jonathan suddenly brightens up. He turns to Indigo and says, "Before you go, there's one last thing I want us to do."

Indigo raises her eyebrows and asks, "What's on your mind, Jonathan?"

Jonathan suggests, "How about one last walk through the park? But this time, let's not just walk—run like children and embrace the freedom of this moment."

Indigo chuckles and nods in agreement, saying, "Why not? Let's make it a race!"

Jonathan and Indigo leap up from the bench and race through the park. They weave through trees and laugh uncontrollably, savoring the moment.

They run into a grassy spot and fall back onto the soft ground, catching their breaths from the laughter. Jonathan suggests, "How about lying on your blanket one last time? I want to soak in this beautiful day."

Indigo spreads the blanket on the grass, and they lie down, gazing up at the sky. As they lie there, Jonathan reaches into his bag and retrieves his journal. He flips it open to a carefully folded note. "I had a feeling you would be leaving soon. So, last night, I drew this for you."

Indigo's eyes sparkle as she unfolds the note. She finds a drawing of the two of them racing through the park with smiles. She looks at Jonathan and says, "Wow, you envisioned us running through the park. I'll cherish the memory." Indigo places the drawing in her journal.

With a sigh, he says, "After I drew us racing, I wrote down a few lessons I am grateful for. I would like you to read them." Jonathan hands her his journal. As Indigo reads his journal, she tears up and smiles.

Jonathan wrote: These are some lessons I have learned during my time with Indigo:

1. Her ability to reflect on your experiences, even amidst nervousness, taught me the value of self-awareness.

2. Thanks to her guidance, I found my passion for counseling at-risk teens and setting clear goals for my future.

3. Through volunteering, she demonstrated that giving time is just as impactful as financial contributions.
4. Her unwavering belief that solutions will appear helped me see possibilities, like our transformative camping trip.
5. The trip also taught me the value of trust, openness, empathy, and owning up to my mistakes.
6. I have started setting a positive example for my younger brother.
7. I have forged a better relationship with my stepfather.

Jonathan says, "I can't thank you enough for helping me to discover my voice. I'm excited to apply these lessons to my journey of self-discovery and helping others."

Indigo closes the journal gently, saying, "Reading this makes me happy. You've understood so much. I thought you were going to forget me."

Jonathan smiles and says, "Indigo, how can I ever forget your smile? I accept my sadness for now. You're like my guardian angel, and I'm sure you'll watch over me."

Indigo chuckles and replies, "I will have the best view. But before you leave, let me give you something I wrote for you last night. Please don't open it until later."

Jonathan accepts the handwritten note from Indigo and carefully places it in his journal. He then takes a photograph of her, wanting to capture this moment forever. Finally, he tightly hugs Indigo. He is overwhelmed with gratitude for the time they've spent together. Jonathan walks away.

Indigo waits until Jonathan is out of sight and packs everything into her backpack. She contacts Bríg in the fourth dimension and sends her backpack to her. Indigo thanks Bríg for the memorable camping trip. Before turning into a shimmering indigo light, she savors her last moment in the third dimension. Indigo is finally ready to depart. She merely thinks of Serenity Haven and finds herself back in the familiar hues of the fifth dimension.

The indigo light sees a violet light and telepathically asks, "Mom, how did I do?"

The violet light responds, "Indigo, you did amazing."

"I missed Serenity Haven. But it is so strange because I will now miss that dimension. Regardless, I am glad I met Jonathan," the indigo light replies.

The violet light says, "You realize you were never alone there. I wish the inhabitants knew that they were never alone. Despite the struggles you faced, your light was very bright."

The violet light floats over to the screen. "Look at the screen. This is Jonathan's past, present, and future. You altered his present, and now he has a different future. His consciousness has increased. Not only did you affect his life, but you have affected the lives of the other inhabitants."

The indigo light brightens, "Thanks, Mom."

"I was watching you also," the indigo light's twin says.

The indigo light asks, "Really?"

"Of course, I was watching. I did have my doubts. I was concerned because you went into a dimension that is so dense. I didn't think you could make a difference there. But, you know, I am pessimistic," the twin says.

The indigo light replies, "Yes, I know you are."

The indigo's light father, a bright aqua light, floats towards her and says, "You did well. I watched your struggles. Yet, you stay focused and overcome the challenges of that realm."

The indigo light says, "I am going to rest. The journey was very emotional. I will go enjoy my quiet time in the crystal." The indigo light floats to her crystal pod and rests.

Meanwhile, in the third dimension, Jonathan is lying down. He takes out his phone to look at Indigo's picture. Instead of seeing Indigo, he sees a bright indigo light. He thinks, "That's strange. She always talked about the inner light or aura."

He reads her note and chuckles, "She is so wise."

For a quick moment, Jonathan thinks, "I wonder if she was investigating someone or if she was here helping me?" He places the note back in his notebook.

✳

Seven years later, the indigo light looks through the holographic display to see how Jonathan is doing. Indigo sees Jonathan has opened a teen center that runs when school is out. She looks around the center and sees vision boards, financial planners, and a computer center. There is a board that has a schedule for volunteering within the community.

The indigo light is amazed at the center. She listens to Jonathan tell a group of four teenagers about her. He is taking them on a trip to Pictured Rocks Lakeshore Park. Before he goes, he gives each teenager a notebook. Inside the notebook, he has placed loose papers summarizing the message Indigo wrote for him.

Jonathan drives the group to the park. He does the same trust exercises with his group. Indigo excitedly watches the camping trip. On the last morning of the camping trip, Jonathan has the group gather by the amazing cove. They go around in a circle and read the note he placed in their notebook.

"I know there might be times when life feels like a puzzle with missing pieces or a maze with no exit. But guess what? The power to unlock those answers, to find your way through the maze, is already within you."

1. Think of it like this: Inside each of you is a treasure chest filled with incredible potential, with dreams waiting to be chased and talents waiting to be uncovered. The key to unlocking that chest is called self-discovery.

2. Let Go of Your Backpack: Sometimes, we carry these invisible backpacks full of burdens and doubts. It can be the baggage of past mistakes, the weight of other people's expectations, or even the fear of failing. Take a deep breath and gently set that backpack down. We can learn from our mistakes without carrying them forever.

3. Gratitude is Your Magic Key: Even when things get tough, there's always something to be thankful for. When you open your heart to gratitude, you unlock a hidden door to new possibilities.

4. Planting Seeds of Growth: Imagine your life like a garden. You must prepare the soil and nurture the seeds to bloom flowers. That means feeding your mind with wisdom and knowledge, challenging yourself to grow, and caring for your well-being.

5. Love Takes the Wheel: Fear and love are the two driving forces in the world. Choose

love. Let it guide your choices, actions, and interactions with others."

6. Seeing Beyond the Tunnel: Sometimes, we get so focused on our immediate surroundings that we forget to look at the bigger picture. Remember, the world is vast and filled with possibilities. Open your mind to new experiences, listen to different perspectives, and trust your intuition.

7. Changing the World, One Step at a Time: We can't control everything around us, but we can control ourselves. Every positive choice and act of kindness makes the world a better place.

8. Remember, the treasure hunt for your best self is an adventure. Enjoy the journey, learn from every step, and never stop unlocking the incredible potential within you.

After the group reads the writings, they have a group hug. Jonathan opens up his backpack and gives each teenager a book. The cover of the book is the one he drew on the camping trip with Indigo and Bríg. The title of his

book is "Dare to Find Your Voice by Knowing Thyself."
He tells the group that he is the main character. As they end
their camping trip and go back to Chicago, Indigo sees
Jonathan's indigo light shining. She knows he has
positively changed his course and the course of others.

Made in the USA
Las Vegas, NV
10 July 2024

92128112R00066